Cold Calling Mastery

Cold Calling Mastery

The Professional Advisor's Guide to Selling Everywhere from Wall Street to Main Street

Scott Pace

Sidecar Press

Cover designed by Chris Meier.

Published in the United States of America by Sidecar Press.

ISBN: 0692257225
ISBN-13: 978-0692257227

DEDICATION

This book is dedicated to every advisor who wants to achieve greatness. I am honored that you have allowed me to help you on this journey.

CONTENTS

ACKNOWLEDGMENTS

To my daughters: your inspiration and humor bring me joy every day. You have given meaning to my life that I have had no right to expect. Always live life as if it's rigged in your favor.

To my editor, John Sherer: thank you for believing in me. Without your support and persistence, this book may not have come to fruition.

To my parents: your love and support are unsurpassed. Even though we're not allowed to pick our parents, if I could have, I wouldn't have changed a thing.

1 INTRODUCTION

When I was six years old, I had my first and (fortunately) only run-in with the law. A police officer came to our school one day to tell us about 9-1-1: what it was for, and how to use it if something ever happened. I went home, got bored, and decided I'd try it out. When the operator asked me what my emergency was, I pretended to be a lady who had taken a bunch of pills.

She obviously believed me because, of course, I had not reached puberty and my voice hadn't dropped. After she asked me several questions I started to get scared, so I hung up. They immediately called back and informed me that you can't hang up on 9-1-1. As I tried to assure them that everything was going to be fine because I was feeling better, they still managed to keep me on the phone. Soon enough they had traced the call, and the doorbell rang.

According to my father, three police officers asked him if a woman in the house had called 9-1-1. He told them that was impossible, since only he and his son were there.

Before I knew it my bedroom door opened, and there were the officers with my father. I was busted. The police gave me a long lecture about why it was wrong to prank call the emergency services. I was scared to death that my poor six-year-old body would be hurled into jail. But somehow, they must have felt sorry for me because they started blaming the officer who had come to the school. He had to return the next day and explain to the class that you should never call 9-1-1 unless you were in a true emergency. The teacher and the principal glared at me with their arms crossed throughout the entire lecture.

Little did they know that this would be the beginning of a long prank calling career, which didn't end until I was in college. I tell you this story because I believe it was, ironically enough, my first official cold call. And although this childish prank had little in common with the hundreds of thousands of cold calls I later made in my career, I think I got the bug to use the phone very early.

Cold calling has a bad reputation. But whether people realize it or not, they usually make several cold calls per week in their personal lives, perhaps to set up a doctor's appointment or to make a restaurant reservation. In business, cold calling is an essential skill for any position, regardless of whether you're a salesperson. It's true that cold calling is not the sexiest job. Rather, it is the grunt work of business. If it's done correctly, however, it can be one of the most lucrative and personally rewarding positions in any industry.

One of the great things about cold calling is its low cost. When you build a business, you typically don't have a big marketing budget or the luxury of waiting for referrals, so if you don't seek out clients, you will be out of business. It may be rough at first, but the more licks you take, the better and stronger you get. If you use the strategies in this book, you'll take fewer licks and see faster results.

Regardless of how long you've been in business, you still have to make cold calls. In the early days of your practice, you may spend the majority of your day on the phone, but even a veteran advisor must master this skill. The most elite advisor who contacts a referral may be technically making a warm call, but the skills required to call a stranger are the same.

Real cold calling is not sitting in a boiler room, turning and burning clients. It's the first knock on the door to building a relationship. It's the process of transforming a complete stranger—a cold prospect—into a warm prospect, which can lead to an appointment.

Why Cold Calling?

I have made millions of dollars during my career, first and foremost through cold calling. I've done it through dedication, hard work, and a commitment to continually improving my techniques. But it didn't happen right away. In fact, my first year in real estate, long before I entered financial services, was nearly a disaster.

Like many who enter a new profession, I was clueless. I was in my early 20s, fresh out of college, and it was my first day in real estate. I walked around the office, took note of what people were doing, and listened to the war stories of older agents who were no longer producing enough income to merit their own offices.

After a few months, I realized that I was on the fast track to nowhere and that I needed a plan. After stumbling on some training materials I had received from a top-producing agent in the office, I was soon introduced to the practice of cold calling.

I have to admit that at first, things weren't pretty. I can recall only one experience from my efforts, and that was rejection. Sure, I used the scripts that were provided and I targeted specific markets that I thought would be interested in my services, but time after time I ended up with no results. The one thing I can say about that experience was that it taught me the discipline to stay on the phone and to keep feeding my hunger for mastering the craft of sales.

In my studies, I came across one of the top agents in the industry. The guy was marvelous. He had a charming Southern accent, and his passion for the industry was addictive. After hearing him speak at a conference, I knew I had to get to know him.

After repeatedly calling his office, which was halfway across United States, he finally took my call. I'll never forget the first thing he said to me: "Scott Pace, what in the Hell can I do for you?"

I told him my story, which I think made him feel sorry for me, and he invited me to a seminar he was putting on in Atlanta. He said he would waive the fee for the seminar if I could find my way there. That was the beginning of an amazing relationship.

I completely engrossed myself in everything he said, and he taught me some very simple techniques for selling over the phone. More importantly, he showed me how to become a machine. That next year, I increased my sales by over 700% and received a prestigious award from my firm. From that point on, I remained in the top 1% of agents in my state. I never looked back.

After leaving the real estate business and venturing into a couple of other of entrepreneurial endeavors, I made my way to Wall Street. When I got licensed I was told that only one in ten survives in the business, but I knew I had one thing that no one else did: my skill set and experiences in cold calling, negotiating, and presenting.

Today, I have enjoyed a celebrated career on Wall Street. As a partner in one of the top wealth management teams in the country, and as the head of business development at both a top-ranked institutional investment firm and an investment consulting firm, I developed a reputation as the guy who could get a meeting with anyone.

While working in the industry, many friends and colleagues asked me how they could better hone their business development skills. Witnessing their success and the life-changing results they achieved in their practices as a result of my guidance, I became addicted to coaching. Dozens of colleagues requested that I write a book, and after leading a training seminar one day, the chairman of my firm told me that he thought I had missed my calling.

I then decided to take all of my experience in sales, marketing, and relationship management, and put it to work helping advisors and firms grow their businesses to tremendous levels. As a result, Advisor Growth was born.

Part of that effort resulted in this book. I wanted to give advisors a handbook on cold calling—one that I wish had existed when I began two decades ago. I wanted it to be a book for beginners as well as veteran advisors. I wanted it to be concise and as free of jargon as possible. An overwhelming majority of books written for business are too long. They inflate 30 pages of material into 300. One of my chief aims here is to give you a succinct guide to cold calling—a condensation of over 20 years of experience—that will expedite your success with as much information in as little space as possible.

"It is one thing to study war and another to live the warrior's life."   —Telamon of Arcadia

If you apply what you've learned in this book correctly, it will be life-changing, not only for you and your business, but also for those closest to you. You will be happier, more financially secure, and more efficient with your time.

In this book, we're going to cover:

- How to set yourself up for success, including how to organize your environment.
- How to build rapport faster than you ever thought possible.
- How to communicate your value and benefits in a matter of seconds.
- How to stay relevant and follow up with prospects, plus thoughts on frequency and strategy.
- The winner's mindset that you must have to be successful.
- Scripts and dialogue, from development to delivery.
- How to handle objections.
- How to use techniques from neuro-linguistic programming (NLP) to connect faster with prospects.
- How to deal with rejection, and a great four-letter word you can use to support a winning mindset.
- The best way to create and manage a pipeline.

I'm looking forward to sharing everything from A to Z that I have learned about cold calling over the past 20 years. If you apply this knowledge, you will become one of the most successful cold calling prospectors in your field. Let's begin.

2 SET-UP

The first and, of course, most important thing we need to talk about is setting yourself up to win. This all begins with creating the right environment. Your environment has to be your sanctuary, your war room, the place where you can go in solitude without interruptions to get on the phone and take care of business.

Your prospecting time is to be scheduled on your daily calendar and treated as an appointment, whether you have scheduled two hours of prospecting per day, four hours, or however much time works for you. It must be treated with no interruptions, the same as an appointment with your most important client. Teach your staff not to distract you during this time. Put a "Do Not Disturb" sign on your door if you have to. Turn your computer off. There will always be trivial matters that threaten to pull you away from prospecting, the lifeblood of your business. Keep them out! Short of your wife going into labor, you must admit no disruptions. Control your business; don't let your business control you.

Tools of the Trade

You need the right hardware: a great telephone and a great headset. I recommend the best headset money can buy because your sound quality is a vital part of how the public perceives you. Every time I get a new headset—of which I've probably had 20—I ask people how I come across on the other end to make sure I don't sound like I'm speaking in a tin can.

Next, you need your appointment book close. I recommend an appointment book that sits on your desk, rather than one on the computer; computers can be very distracting, from email to the news that comes across the wire. You don't want anything stealing your attention. After you set appointments in your book, you can then transfer them to your computer. Furthermore, a hard copy is always useful to have around the office, for instance, if you're on the road and your assistant cannot, for whatever reason, access the electronic information.

We will cover the specifics later, but you also need to have an amazing script that you can always go back to if you get off course. I have used hundreds of scripts throughout my career, but no matter how many times I have used a particular script, I always keep a copy of it at my fingertips.

The last thing you need is a well-defined, scrubbed list of prospects to call. I recommend finding a company that can provide you with the highest-quality leads that are relevant to your calling campaign. If you cut corners and purchase a list of leads from a non-reputable source, it will be like fishing in a pond with few to no fish in it. You will spend more time dialing and not reaching people (or not reaching the qualified people you seek) than if you were randomly picking people out of the phone book. Trust me, find a great source for your leads; it is one of the most efficient things you can do. Your firm probably has the names of some reputable sources. If not, contact my office; I'll be more than happy to give you the name of a great source that I used for years.

Further Tips

Some additional thoughts on setting up your environment are as follows. First is the importance of taking breaks. I recommend ten-minute break every hour. If you decide to venture out of your office, don't let people bother you with supposedly urgent but actually unimportant issues that can take you out of your mental state. If you can, stay in your office unless you need to use the restroom, but then get back as soon as possible. It's fine to listen to some music, get up and stretch, or just relax; but by no means is this an opportunity for you to check emails and voicemails. All of that will be waiting for you when you're done with your prospecting session.

Second, I recommend that if you're cold calling for the first time in your career, you should work your way up to longer sessions. Don't start with four hours of daily cold calling, even if you have little else to do during the day. If you're new to the business, consider beginning with one hour per day and increasing your time steadily. Cold calling zaps more energy than you might expect, and if you haven't done much of it before, you will be too worn out to attend to other business during the workday.

A final tip, also for newcomers: don't be afraid to get on the phone and make mistakes. It's inevitable that you will fumble from time to time. You may even throw up on some people, metaphorically speaking. Believe me, I have my own horror stories from when I first started, but through practice and repetition, I became one of the best cold callers in the industry. Think of yourself as an actor: you learn to speak your lines naturally by saying them over and over. It probably won't sound effortless the first time. Mistakes are part of the process; you will learn from them and get better.

3 MINDSET

What is your attitude about cold calling, your set of beliefs, your frame of reference? Attitudes usually come from experiences. For example, if you have a daily ritual of going to the gym, chances are you have a pretty positive attitude about it. Although at times it may be painful or uncomfortable, you still derive pleasure from the results you get. Maybe it's better health, maybe it's a better physique—either way, the results and potential results outweigh any discomfort.

I bring this up because reluctance about cold calling usually comes from a series of bad experiences in one's career. That's why so many never spend much time on it or stop before they see success. Early in my career, I dealt with rejection after rejection, and the only thing that kept me going was the occasional positive call that led to an appointment. If I had not ignored all the rejection, I would not have been able to take control of my career.

The Belief Cycle

Belief influences outcome. Let me provide an illustration of how this works. I call it the "belief cycle." Imagine a circle with four points in a clockwise sequence: "Belief" is at noon, "Possibility" is at 3:00, "Action" is at 6:00, and "Outcome" is at 9:00.

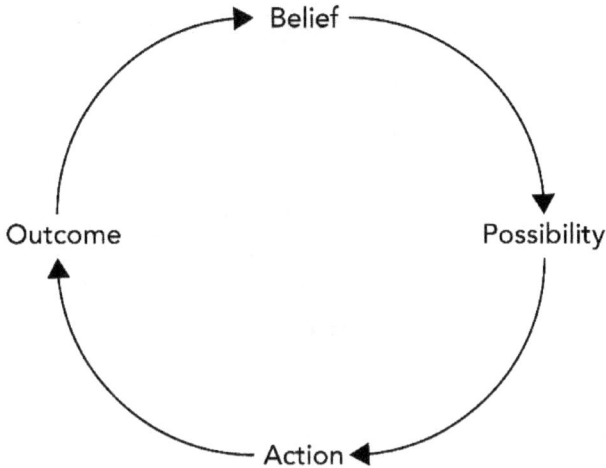

It all starts with belief. If our beliefs about a given task are negative and pessimistic, we will ascribe little possibility to it. That will in turn affect the amount of action we apply to the task. If we apply little action, we're going to end up with few or no results, which will reinforce the negative beliefs that we started with. On the other hand, if we believe that performing a task has great possibility and a high probability of return, we will get excited about it and apply a massive amount of action. When you apply massive amounts of action, you often get unprecedented outcome—once again reinforcing your belief, but this time in a positive way.

Cold calling is an art, but when it comes to your beliefs and your mindset, there is a science to success. This science can be applied to anything in your life; but when you use it for cold calling, as long as you have absolute certainty that it will work and that your methods and techniques are correct, you can then apply a massive amount of action, cut through the rejection, and focus only on the positive results. Doing so will reinforce your beliefs, thereby turning cold calling into a positive and rewarding experience.

Think about the last thing you refused to give up on, the last time you made something an obsession, the last time you burned the ships and forged ahead. I would bet you either found or made a way to success; that is what all of the most successful people in history have done. When you change the way you look at life and the success you can achieve, and when you repudiate complacency, that is the day you will become unstoppable.

Good Practices

After many years of working in the industry and training other advisors, I have noticed that a good cold caller follows a few practices to establish and maintain the proper mindset. If you follow these instructions, cold calling will cease to be a chore and will become a fruitful, even joyful, part of your day.

First and foremost, don't take anything personally. Remember that these people do not know who you are. They don't know what you do for hobbies, how hard you work at your job, or that you're a dedicated spouse or parent.

Second, don't be afraid. Of course, you may be uncomfortable when you're new to cold calling, but if you keep at it, the fear will eventually vanish.

Third, you must have the attitude that you're doing this for the greater good. You're there to help people, not to get into their pocketbooks or simply make a lot of deals. Advising is all about bettering people's positions. If you forget that, you won't get any results, and the job will crush your spirit. Keep in mind that you're looking for people to help, and that *you* decide which clients to do business with. If a prospect is ever mean or rude or calls you a name, remember your higher purpose and move on to the next person who might need your help.

Fourth, be prepared. Know your product and tailor it to the specific group of people you're calling. I've been cold calling for decades, but I still screw up if I don't do my prep work. Don't get overconfident about your ability to wing it.

Fifth, be ready for their objections. We'll cover these in more detail later on, but keep in mind that there are only a handful of objections a prospect will give you. If you are prepared for these few possibilities, a prospect will have to say no several times before you get off the phone, and you will know how to phrase your answers so as to end the conversation in a good way, with permission to contact them again.

Finally, a very important part of this process is making it a ritual. Studies show that it takes 30 consistent days of applying a practice to make it a habit. If you'll commit to applying the techniques and practices in this book for 30 days, it will become second nature.

When you embark on this journey, you have to believe that whatever you do, you will do it to win. Cold calling is a skill like any other—cycling, writing, golf, or chess; the more you practice over time, the better you will become.

Let's now discuss the particulars of how you approach your prospects.

Change Your Approach

Over the years, I have trained a great many advisors on how to be successful in cold calling. One of the most frequent mistakes I see is advisors setting a goal to reach a certain number of individuals every day or to make a certain number of phone calls per day; if they meet that goal, they call it a successful day. Nothing is further from the truth. For some reason, a common goal for many advisors is to make 200 phone calls per day, whether they're calling to set up individual appointments, client events, or prospect events. As a result, they are burnt out and beaten up, and they rarely find enjoyment in their careers.

Every time I meet an advisor in this position, I give them a new challenge, the same one that I'm going to give you now. I challenge you to throw away your call quota and replace it with a new list numbered one through ten. Your new goal is to have ten meaningful conversations with prospects every single day. If you have at least ten meaningful conversations, I promise you that you will find at least one to three appointments or bookings for your event. By focusing on only ten meaningful conversations, it removes the undesirable task of making 100 or 200 phone calls a day. Think about it: how much more exciting would it be to come to the office knowing that you only need to have ten great conversations and that they will result in one to three appointments? Just the thought of it should make you feel less burdened and overwhelmed.

I don't have to explain in much detail what a meaningful conversation is, because I think you know. It's one in which you actually connect with someone on the phone. It's one in which you share information, in which you listen to them, and—just as importantly—in which they actually listen to you. In many cases, it's one that lasts more than five minutes. Connecting with people on the phone helps you see them not as a mere commodity or a means to an end. This, in turn, changes your energy and the way they perceive you.

When you get on the phone, it's your job to make a

friend, build rapport, and find a way to help. If you believe that you're calling to help them better their situation, you will find that you are received in a much more positive light. Even now, when I pick up the phone to make a cold call, I tell myself: I am only making a handful of calls today, and this person just happens to be among the lucky ones. I know that my job is to connect with that person. I know with absolute certainty that the services I provide can improve their circumstances. By believing that, I have now made the most important sale there is: **the sale to myself**.

One of the biggest hindrances I have seen with advisors is, believe it or not, a lack of confidence; they are afraid of rejection and of feeling vulnerable. If you can make the sale to yourself first, you will internalize the right mindset and open yourself to helping a lot of people. They will hear in your voice that you are genuine and trustworthy. If, on the other hand, you're mostly concerned with making money, with wheeling and dealing, be sure that your reputation will suffer, and that you probably won't last very long in your industry.

Another major obstacle you will face when cold calling is this: the person on the other end of the phone is most likely receiving multiple sales calls per day. Whether I'm trying to reach an institution, a business owner, a center of influence, or a private investor, I must differentiate myself by doing two vital things that most cold callers don't do: building rapport and listening. Imagine you're a business owner who has received three calls in the same day from advisors who are quickly running through their scripts, sounding wooden and over-rehearsed. But then a fourth advisor calls, one who sounds genuine, has relevant things to say, and actually listens. Think of how much that fourth advisor will stand out. When cold calling, you have only ten or fifteen seconds to build rapport. We will discuss the specifics of building rapport later, but for now, remember that rapport and listening are the two most important ways to stand out from the crowd.

Know Your Objective

The next principle you want to apply in order to obtain the proper mindset is having a clear objective. It might sound elementary, but time after time I see advisors make the mistake of not having one. I'll ask you right now: when you get on the phone, what is your objective? We already know that we're there to make a friend and build rapport, but after that, what's your objective? I'll tell you: your objective is to get an appointment. After you build rapport and listen to the prospect's responses to your questions, you cannot be afraid to ask for the appointment.

Many advisors get so caught up on "indications of interest" that they lose sight of booking qualified appointments. I often see advisors who love to brag about how many indications of interest they have generated. I ask them, "What qualifies someone to be an indication of interest?" Usually they respond, "Someone who is looking to do business within the next year or two, or perhaps come to a client event." That's paltry; I could get that on every single phone call I make.

In order to avoid the "indications of interest" trap, I urge you to create a system that will help keep your objective—booking appointments—in mind at all times. I suggest that you rank only four categories of prospects:

1) A hot lead, who will make a decision within three months.

2) Someone who will make a decision within three to six months.

3) Someone who will make a decision within six to nine months.

4) Someone who will make a decision within nine to twelve months.

The fourth category is a little tricky, because those who want to make a decision much later are always the most ambivalent. As a result, you should label as a 4 all prospects who seem to be dragging their feet and delaying the process. These are the ones who, because of "unforeseen circumstances," occasionally miss an appointment or fail to return a phone call. They act interested, but life just keeps getting in the way. I know this is a very subjective category, but these people will always delay the process, and the lower they are in the rankings, the easier they are to replace with valid prospects. My goal is to have you spend the majority of your efforts on those you believe you can convert within six months. If you focus your attention on the 1s and 2s, your practice will become more predictable, efficient, and enjoyable.

If you can't categorize prospects based on your intuition, you must rely on what they have verbally communicated to you. If you're speaking to someone about an appointment for a second look or to discuss their IRA or insurance, and they're willing to set up a meeting next month or next quarter, that's a hot lead; you should rank them as such. If someone says, "I'm interested in your client event, but due to scheduling conflicts I can't make it; please contact me about the next one," then that's a hot lead and should be categorized as a 1. If someone says, "We're putting out an RFP next quarter," then that's a hot lead and you need to get over there immediately. From here I'm sure you can create your own examples of how to categorize 2s and 3s.

However, if someone tells you they're not interested and that you should call them back next year, they are *not* an indication of interest. If you fill your pipeline with people who say, "I'll think about it," or, "Check with me next year," you are putting garbage in your pipeline and can expect nothing but garbage to come out. Your job is to find hot and warm leads and convert them to appointments. You want to make sure your pipeline is filled only with people with whom you've had meaningful conversations, and whom you know you will be meeting or converting in less than a year.

You will find that once you develop a great pipeline, you'll spend the first hour or two of your session calling the hot and warm leads. The rest of your calling time can be devoted to true cold calls in order to replenish your pipeline; this will help you replace either the prospects-turned-clients or the 4s who weren't going to convert anyway. That way, you don't have to spend all your time with the cold prospects. It will probably take you at least six months to build a strong pipeline, but when you have one, it will be the foundation of all your new business.

Know Your Audience

Whether you're calling an individual or an institutional prospect, it helps to know what services they may be looking for. The services *you* want to sell *them* do not matter. Once you know what services they seek, make sure your discussion revolves around what will interest them, based on their needs and wants, not your own. Maybe it's tax efficiency, lending, or insurance. Maybe it's outsourced CIO; maybe it's rolling out of their 401(k) plan. In any case, have a set topic that is specific to your audience.

If you call a business owner and want to talk to him about how you can save him time and money by assisting him with his qualified retirement plan or corporate cash management, it will be a much more meaningful conversation than if you were to call about opening an IRA. If you're calling a specific neighborhood or demographic group to set up a seminar, it makes more sense to discuss issues of taxation or trust and estate planning than it might to offer a seminar on hedge funds. I'm sure you get my point; just make sure you have something relevant to your audience when you get on the phone. For some of you, this will be common sense; but believe me, I have seen not only novice but also seasoned cold callers make this mistake.

State Management

Now that we've talked about making a friend, having meaningful, relevant conversations, knowing your audience, selling yourself first with absolute certainty, and having a clear objective, I want to tell you how to combine these factors into a daily ritual that will put you in the proper mindset before you pick up the phone.

The key to this is state management. State management means putting yourself in the state that gives you the most positive emotion, a winning attitude, and keeps you on track so that rejection won't distract you from your mission. Have you ever watched a professional athlete play the game of their life? Remember the days when Michael Jordan couldn't miss a shot? Maybe you've seen your favorite baseball hero hit three home runs in a game. Or if you've ever attended a PGA event, you've noticed how focused and determined a professional golfer's pre-shot ritual is. If you've ever seen something like that, you've witnessed someone getting into their peak emotional state. In countless interviews, top professionals from every occupation have referred to this as "getting in the zone." Once they're in that zone, they feel unstoppable, and that's where I want you to be when you pick up the phone. Just as a top NBA player will spend as much time visualizing free throws as he does physically making them, so should you visualize making cold calls.

After you get into the office, close the door, and accept that this time is just as important as a meeting with a real client, I want you to sit at your desk or stand up (there's no preference), close your eyes, and visualize how you want your calls to go. I want you to visualize dialing the phone. I want you to visualize what the person on the other end may look like. I want you to visualize the two of you smiling during your conversation; I want you to visualize listening to them intently; I want you to visualize them agreeing with what you have to say. I want you to visualize them setting an appointment. I want you to visualize putting the appointment on your calendar. I want you to visualize them becoming a new client. I want you to visualize becoming the number-one advisor at your firm.

During this exercise it's imperative that you see, hear, and feel all of this taking place. Let the feeling of success radiate through your body. Feel the pride, and imagine what it will be like to help this new client. When you do this, make sure your eyes are closed, and put everything you have into it. I know it may sound a little goofy, but believe me, you will get out of it what you put into it. You should spend anywhere from three to five minutes on this exercise. If it helps, play some music in the background to pump yourself up. If all of this is done right, you will be glowing with enthusiasm and kindness, and it will come through in your phone calls.

Where the mind goes, the body will follow. If you believe this in your heart, it will come through in your language, your tone, and your energy. On the other hand, suppose you come into the office irritated because someone almost hit you in traffic and your staff is now asking you to handle a dozen things at once. Skipping your visualization time and getting straight on the phone will prove disastrous; your prospect will detect your bad mood and will not want to work with you, which will only add to your frustration. There have been some days when I have delayed or even canceled my session because my mindset wasn't right; when I forced it, it was a waste of my day. If you do your visualization exercise correctly, I promise you will see a higher rate of success and feel better about your work.

A Four-Letter Word for Rejection

The last thing I want to talk about regarding mindset is rejection. Unfortunately, in the practice of cold calling you will face rejection 70–95% of the time. It's okay—live with it, deal with it. You have to remember that you cannot help everybody. The people who tell you no or hang up on you are doing you and your pipeline a favor; they're not wasting your time or giving you false hopes. They are removing themselves from the process. Don't take it personally—how could you? They don't know who you are; they don't know your story or anything about you. So don't take it to heart. The best four-letter word for rejection that I've ever found is NEXT. That's right, just move on to the next one.

Remember to keep the mindset that your time is so valuable that you only make a handful of calls per day. And remember, some of the greatest baseball players in history were successful only 20–30% of the times they went up to bat. You are only looking for yeses, so don't focus on the noes. What you focus on is what you get. If you have a run of bad calls, take a break and do your visualization exercise again. Then get back on the phone and go to work. In my career, I've gone one or two days without generating a lead. You can imagine, or perhaps you know from experience, how discouraging that is. But the funny thing was that the next day, I would end up setting two or three appointments in the first hour. The key when that happens is not to over-celebrate. Be happy and be grateful, but more importantly, use the momentum of your success to make more calls. Keep your head up, believe in yourself and your service, and go help some people.

4 ON THE PHONE

With the proper mindset in place, we can put it to work. Cold calling is an art, not a science. If implemented correctly, everything that you've learned up to this point and are about to learn will cut years off your learning curve and skyrocket your success.

Cold calling is a necessary skill. Whether you prospect daily to set meetings or client events, or just occasionally pick up the phone to reach out to someone with whom you've never spoken, all of these techniques will enhance your probability for success. People always ask me, "How on earth did you get that meeting?" or "That restaurant is booked months in advance; how did you get a reservation?" It's because I build rapport quickly to make a friend, and we all know that friends like helping friends. As I said before, cold calling is not just a business skill; all of the strategies and techniques in this book have become second nature to me and have permeated into other areas of my life.

Let me give you an example. Let's say you want to book a reservation at a popular restaurant. Consider whether you'll be more successful by calling to ask them if they have availability on Friday night at 7:00, or by doing something like the following. Let's assume the name of the woman who answers the phone is Sarah. I might begin with something like this: "Sarah, hi, it's Scott Pace, how are you?" I would then wait for her to respond as if we knew each other, and mentally I'm assuming that as well, even though we've never met. Next I would ask, "Are you guys staying busy?" After her response I would say, "I've got a special dinner on Friday night and have been bragging about you guys. I was wondering if you could fit me in for a table for four at 7:00." Regardless of whether they're booked or not, I'm successful probably 95% of the time.

Do you see what I did here? I built rapport immediately, which helped me gain credibility and separated me from everyone else who has called. I paid them a great compliment, and I aligned my interest with theirs by wanting to expose their business to new people. Then I made my request, which probably made her feel like she was doing an old friend a favor. Now, this book is not about making reservations, but you can see how the right language, attitude, and mindset can get you a lot further on the phone—not only at work, but in life.

Building Rapport

Before we get into scripts, dialogue, overcoming objections, and how to be relevant, I want to share with you a secret I learned close to 20 years ago. I want to tell you about NLP, which stands for neuro-linguistic programming. NLP is the process of modeling the patterns of human behavior, the process through which we perceive, know, and learn things about others. It's a fact that people like people who are like them, so if we can mirror and match them through pitch, tone, and speed, it gives us a chance to build rapport much faster, whether in person or over the phone. This is true because in many cases—especially with scripts—it's not what you say, but how you say it.

For example, if I get anyone on the phone who has a heavy accent, I will do my best, without sounding obvious, to incorporate a few very subtle elements of their speech pattern into mine. If someone speaks really fast, I will speak fast. If someone speaks slowly, I will speak slowly. If someone is loud, I will be loud. And if they're soft, I will be soft. If you're speaking with a woman you may want to consider speaking a little softer, but only if the woman speaks softer—not all women do. Most importantly, do not be condescending to anyone and *do not* make it obvious. I'll never forget a meeting I had a few years ago in Dallas. After a very pleasant appointment with a female prospect, she looked at me on our way to the door and said, "You know, I get a lot of calls for meetings every week." I laughed and replied, "I'm sure you do; what made you decide to meet with me?" She told me that she like the sound of my voice and that I sounded genuine. This is just an example of how proper mirroring and matching can be effective in setting an appointment with anyone.

People like people who are like them. I know this may sound odd, but if you do it correctly and don't exaggerate, it is effective nearly 100% of the time at building rapport. When you get on the phone, within five to ten seconds the person on the other end is starting to judge you, so you have to do your best to be likeable and build rapport as soon as possible. Think of yourself as a chameleon. You have to adapt to your environment and your audience on every call. This works for the same reason that you have similar interests with your friends; the more someone feels that you are similar to them, the more they will like and accept you.

This is an exercise you should practice in your face-to-face meetings as well. To that end, I'm going to give you a challenge. The next time you meet a complete stranger, I want you to mirror their gestures and body language, their tonality, and the speed of their speech. I guarantee you that that person will act more open and friendly in your presence. If you don't believe me, just give it a try. This is one of the greatest secrets I can share with you; please don't overlook it. It gave me the reputation on Wall Street as the guy who could get an appointment with anyone, anywhere. To this day, when I pull up to a hotel I haven't been to in a year, the doorman remembers my name. Part of the reason is that I make everyone I come in contact with my friend, and it all starts with NLP.

When you're on the phone your job is to build rapport and gain credibility fast. After you do that, you then have permission to state your value and why it's relevant, and only then to ask for the close.

In addition to NLP, let me give you three other quick ways to build rapport and gain credibility. One way is to give them a compliment; this usually causes people to let their guard down. Maybe it's a compliment on their business or, when you meet them in person, on their clothing.

A second way is to drop the name of someone you know in common. This builds credibility and helps establish trust, even though you may never have met the person you're calling.

A third way is to agree with a statement they make. You want to align yourself with them and their needs. Never get caught up in some petty dispute, even if the other person is rude. Your ultimate goal on the phone is to set a meeting, so don't be argumentative or combative. I've built hundreds of relationships over the years that started with a bad phone call; these people were difficult at first, but I was able to reach out to them again because I didn't burn any bridges. Sometimes you have to agree with what they say to align yourself with their best interests and show that you are there to help them.

How Do I Write a Script?

I have found that it's not always what you say in a script, but how you say it. So as we discuss how to construct a script, or if you choose to use the ones I provide, be sure to make them your own. In other words, you have to practice them over and over again so that they become second nature. That way, it won't sound like you're reading a script, but having a meaningful conversation with the prospect. Practicing your scripts will not only make you more confident, but will also give you certainty—and certainty is what sells.

Scripts are funny things. They constantly need to be revised and adapted for the audience that you're calling. You obviously cannot use the same script for calling an institution as you would for trying to book a seminar for soon-to-be retirees. This may seem like common sense, but over the years I have seen many advisors make the mistake of not considering the nature of each prospect. I'm going to provide you with scripts that cover many audiences; just remember that if you want to have a relevant conversation, your script should match your market. Whether you cold call in the financial services industry, the insurance industry, or any other professional advising industry, use these scripts as a template and adapt them to your particular services and offerings.

Someone told me years ago never to ask how someone is doing when greeting them on a sales call. I completely disagree. Admittedly, if you ask someone how they are doing, they will give you a cursory answer in most cases, but they almost always ask you how you are doing in return as a kind of reflex. This gives you an opportunity to engage them in a conversation about something relevant to the moment. You might comment on the weather, the market, a holiday weekend, your seasonal allergies kicking in, or a big sports game from the night before. Even if they then respond for no other reason than politeness, you are still building rapport, and it can be a great segue into your script. The sample scripts that follow omit this step for the sake of brevity, but don't forget that you should start getting to know the prospect through conversation even before beginning your script.

A proper script has five elements:

1) It tells who you are.
2) It tells what you do.
3) It tells who you do it for.
4) It tells how your product or service will benefit them.
5) It asks to set an appointment.

So a sample script for a **business owner** might look like this:

Hi _____, I am _____ with _____. We work with (type of client) to (your service), so they can (client benefits).

I'm going to be in (city) on (date). If you have some time that day, I would like to get together with you and show you how I can (provide benefit) for you. And _____, when we meet, I promise you it will be well worth your time.

Notice how this example meets all the criteria. Now, here is an actual script I have used in the past:

Hi John, I am Scott with _____. We work with business owners to streamline their companies' retirement plans and remove the day-to-day investment burden that their HR departments face, so that they can focus more time on the growth and prosperity of their businesses. I'm going to be in your area of town next week visiting clients, and if you have a few moments on Tuesday or Wednesday, I would enjoy the opportunity to meet you. And John, when we get together, I promise you, it will be well worth your time.

That script takes all of about 20–25 seconds to get through. If done correctly, it will secure you an appointment with any business owner who faces the challenges you mentioned in your script. You want your script to be as broad as possible, so that you're not pigeon-holing your services or specifying something that the prospect may not need.

Here is another:

Hi Alex, this is Scott with _____. We specialize in working with business owners and senior executives. I assist them with complex needs in the areas of concentrated stock options, restricted securities, deferred compensation, and estate-planning. I would like to get together with you and share some strategies that we are currently implementing with our clients. I have a couple of times available next week on Tuesday or Thursday. What time is better for you?

Let's look at another for an **individual investor:**

Hi Mary, this is Scott Pace with ABC Advisors. We specialize in providing comprehensive retirement planning so individual investors just like you will not run out of money in retirement. I am available next week on Tuesday and Thursday. If you have time in your calendar, I would really enjoy meeting you.

This is very non-threatening and lets them know you are there to help. The key is always to make the prospect feel comfortable; you must assure them that you know what you're talking about.

Here is another:

Hi Matt, this is Scott Pace with ABC Advisors. Are you familiar with us? We specialize in comprehensive investment strategies so our clients can have peace of mind that they will not run out of funds in retirement.

If you have 15–20 minutes next week, I would enjoy getting together with you. The least that will happen is that you will come away with one or two ideas that we are implementing with our clients right now. And if what we do is not a fit at this time, I at least want you to view me as a trusted resource for anything you may need in the future.

I have used the example of having enough money for retirement because it's a basic one, but you can always adapt it to whatever topic you want. Just make sure it's relevant for your prospects.

Below are a few examples you could use for a **center of influence**. When calling a center of influence, remember to emphasize that you want to collaborate with them. This is not about making a sale; it's about helping them. Only after you help them will they want to help you. Good centers of influence get multiple calls per day from people looking to "help their clients." Rarely do they get a call from someone who wants to bring them new business. Consider the following:

> Hi William, I'm Scott Pace with ABC Advisors. I understand you are one of the top CPAs in town. Tax efficiency is always a topic of conversation when I meet with my clients. You have a great reputation in the industry, and I would like to get together with you in person to learn a little bit more about your practice and see if there might be an opportunity to collaborate with some clients. I'm asked for recommendations for great CPAs from time to time, and I would like to have someone I can refer them to, someone I know and trust, who is also familiar with how I work with my clients.

You want to run through this script completely before you give them a chance to reply. If you enter the relationship as a collaborator and not as a salesperson (because you're there to enhance their business), it's hard for them to turn you down.

However, when getting to know centers of influence, I highly recommend that you break it up into three meetings. Let the first meeting be all about them and their business, then the second can be about you and your business. The third meeting can just be a social event, since you really want to get to know the person. Schedule the first meeting at their office, and come prepared with a list of questions, for example:

- What inspired you to get into the business?
- What kinds of clients do you serve?
- What does your ideal client look like?
- What challenges do they face?
- If we work together, what could I do to make your job easier?

Don't say too much about what you do until the second meeting. If they inquire about your business during the first meeting, just use that as an opportunity to set the second one: ask them if they have time to come to your office next week. When they get there, give them a tour. If you have a cubicle instead of an office, take them to a conference room. Bring them coffee or some water. This is your opportunity to tell them about what you do, but keep the conversation focused on how you can help them by working with mutual clients. The third meeting should be an opportunity to spend some time together outside either of your offices. This may be a lunch or breakfast meeting, or perhaps you invite them to a sporting event. Remember that you want to build not only an alliance, but also a friendship that is a little beyond a professional relationship. No one will refer you business if they don't know, like, and trust you.

Centers of influence are professionals, just like you. They're looking to work with people who won't give them career risk. You need to be very competent in your field, and you need to demonstrate that to them. They know it will reflect poorly on them if you are not an exemplary advisor to the clients they refer you. Few things will destroy your reputation faster than jeopardizing their relationships with their clients.

Here is one of my favorite and most effective scripts for setting an appointment with a center of influence:

> Hi Amy, this is Scott Pace with XYZ Advisors. We have mutual clients in Mr. and Mrs. Arnold. In working with them, it has dawned on me that we have never had the opportunity to meet. I hear wonderful things about you and would love to hear more about your practice to see if you might be a good fit for some of my other clients. When would be a time we could get together?

That script alone is worth the price of admission. Whether you have 10 clients or 100 clients, you are sitting on a gold mine. If you haven't asked all of them who their other advisors are—their accountants, trust attorneys, business attorneys, etc.—and pursued relationships with these other advisors, then you have massive opportunities left to explore. If you can befriend three to five good centers of influence and reciprocate business, you will have an evergreen of introductions and referrals for the rest of your career. Do a great job for them, make them look good, take care of them, and reward them. Pursuing friendships with centers of influence can easily lead to a 20–30% increase in your business every year.

Scripts for **seminars** are also important to have in your toolbox. Some advisors have moved away from targeting neighborhoods when booking seminars, but they can still be a fruitful source. Another great source is companies; many advisors now target large firms in their cities, whether they're engineering firms, telecom firms, manufacturing firms, or whatever happens to be nearby. Again, adapt these scripts for the services you provide.

Here is an example for a seminar aimed at engineers for a particular firm:

> Hello, I'm Scott Pace with XYZ Advisors. We are one of the top wealth management groups in town, and we specialize in working with engineers like you.
>
> You've probably read or seen a lot of debate on the topic of rising interest rates. Due to a large demand, we are holding a lunch discussing how to prepare for and protect your retirement portfolio not if, but when this does occur.
>
> Of course, since you work at _____, this is completely free and you are welcome to bring guests such as a spouse, business partner, coworker, or even your neighbor—anyone that you feel may be affected by this topic.
>
> Our highlighted speaker will be _____. This is open only to a limited number of guests, and I have four spots left. Would you like to join us?

Notice how I mentioned there were only four spots available. This helps create urgency. A script like this is a great opportunity to expand your audience through introductions. If the prospect says yes, ask them if they have a business partner, colleague, friend, or neighbor who might be interested in attending. Then get that person's contact information, and when you make the next call, use the first prospect's name to establish rapport and break the ice.

An easy thing to do when you're trying to book seminars is to tell your prospects that the event will be based around some list. Maybe you're hosting a seminar on the top five mistakes you see investors making before retirement. Maybe it's on the three most important things to know about life insurance. Whatever the topic, lists provide a compelling reason for people to pay attention.

Here is another example:

> Hello, I'm Scott Pace with XYZ Advisors. We specialize in advising many of the employees at your company, so we know firsthand the issues and concerns they have in preparing for retirement. We are hosting an event on Tuesday to discuss 401(k) rollover options. If you're interested in coming, there is limited space available, but since we haven't had the opportunity to meet, I wanted to make it a priority to give you the chance to attend.

Are you seeing a pattern here? Tell them who you are, what you do, whom you do it for, and how it benefits them; then close. You can use these scripts as they are, or take bits and pieces from different ones to create hybrids. Either way, you have to make them your own; you must internalize them and practice them over and over. They have to roll off your tongue like you're singing your favorite song. Your delivery will be the key to your success because people will hear the confidence and certainty in your voice.

One final tip that I give many advisors is that they should not end their sentences on a vocal upswing. Raising the pitch at the end makes you sound uncertain and less confident, almost like you're asking a question. When ending your sentences, use a normal tone or one that's deeper than when you began.

5 OBJECTIONS

Objections are always important when discussing sales. In more than 20 years in sales and marketing, I have found five primary reasons for why prospects raise objections:

1) Lack of trust
2) Lack of time
3) Lack of money
4) Lack of need
5) The real buyer was not identified

Most of these are self-explanatory, so if you feel a roadblock when you're trying to build a relationship, do your best to identify which of these may be the cause. The only way to find out is through asking questions; the questions in the next chapter are especially useful in furthering a conversation, whether by countering an objection or opening a dialogue. We'll go over these questions in more detail, but for now, let's focus on the objections you will face.

Trust is developed with time. The prospect must feel that your priorities are aligned with theirs and that you truly care about bettering their situation. If they don't feel these things, you're wasting your time and you'll never close with anyone. Remember that the more someone trusts you, and the more they feel a personal connection with you, the fewer objections you will face. Some relationships take longer than others, but one indicator of trust is when a prospect begins to volunteer information that you did not ask about. When this happens, you will know you're on the path to building a solid, trusting relationship.

If their objection is about **time**, they don't consider you a relevant priority. If their objection is about **money**, then you have not shown them examples of opportunity loss—the pain related to not making a change. If they object on the grounds of **need**, then you have not uncovered enough pain—either known or unknown to the client—in their current situation. People buy on emotion, and logic helps them justify it. When people buy, they believe that their needs and wants will be fulfilled, so when they ask themselves if it's worth it, their answer must be yes—it must be worth their time and effort.

Your job is to demonstrate that they will experience more pain in their current situation than if they make a change. Buying from you is pleasure; not buying will prolong the pain or may have unintended consequences. Don't tell them what it will cost them not to change, but ask them questions that will lead them to express in their own words what could happen if they don't take action. When people formulate the answer and hear it in their own words, it resonates deeper with them. For example, if I tell you that you will gain weight by eating doughnuts, it will have a weaker effect than if I ask you what will happen if you continue eating them; when you answer that you will probably gain weight, you will be more likely to take responsibility for your actions and change your behavior accordingly.

A final reason for objections that I often see, especially when marketing to institutions, is that sometimes **advisors do not identify the real economic buyer**, the one who will either write the check or sign off on the project. For this reason, during your discovery process you must identify which members of the committee are the decision-makers and focus your efforts on them; always ask who else will be part of the decision-making process. If you are a financial advisor, do not be stopped by anyone who works in human resources. They do a valuable job organizing benefits and payroll, and they may be well-versed in insurance, but they usually know nothing about investing. Too often, HR representatives get in the way of decisions that should really be made by the CFO, CIO, or others on the investment committee. The buck does not stop with HR, so don't let them be the gatekeepers for your clients' investment decisions. Never accept a "no" from someone who doesn't have the authority to give you a "yes."

In addition to these general categories of objections, here are some more specific objections that advisors commonly encounter on the phone and the most effective rebuttals for them.

1) I'm already working with an advisor.

Chances are good that you have heard this more than once. As always, tailor my responses to your industry, but here's my best answer for when you encounter this objection:

> That's great! I would be very surprised if you weren't working with an advisor. As a matter of fact, most of our clients were working with an advisor when we met them. I just wanted to get together with you in person and show you some of our services that distinguish us in the marketplace. Plus, it is always prudent to get a second opinion on your investment portfolio. Believe me, you would be surprised at some of the things we

have come across, especially in terms of fees, risk, and prudent investment choices. I have some time on my calendar next week if you're available, and I promise you it would be well worth your time.

You may already have a similar response to this objection. Just remember that a few things set apart a cold caller who handles objections well from one who doesn't: body language, tone of voice, NLP, and a sincere demonstration of willingness to help—in other words, the same things we have been talking about so far.

2) I don't have any time to see you.

This is quite common, because at this point you're not a priority to the prospect. Just agree with them and say:

I understand you're busy—most successful people are—but I'm very interested in meeting with you. If you can give me a couple of times on your calendar when you might be available, even for 10 or 15 minutes, I will work around your schedule.

This shows that you consider them a priority and will do whatever it takes to get in the door.

3) I'm just not interested.

When cold calling, this will probably be your most frequent objection. Just say:

I totally understand. I would simply like to get

together with you in person and introduce myself, so that if you have any future needs, I will be at the top of your list of advisors.

At this point, people usually say that they're already working with an advisor, so you can then respond accordingly.

4) We're not looking to make a change right now.

I used to get this a lot when prospecting for institutional business, but you can use it for private clients as well. You can respond:

> I completely understand. If you were, it would be great timing on my part! I would actually just like to get together with you and share some of the strategies we are implementing with our clients right now, so when the time comes to consider a change, you will be familiar with our services. Are you available next Tuesday or Thursday?

This lets them know that you're aware of their situation and that you want to open the door to becoming a resource for them. Developing institutional relationships can take years, so don't be discouraged if you have to get to know them gradually.

5) Just send me some information.

When you get this one, you will have to use your discretion as to whether it's worth sending them information. If you don't, you could be sending fifty packets per day. With a business or institution, you could say:

> I'm actually going to be near you later this week. Would it be okay if I stopped by and delivered it? That way, I could introduce myself in person.

Very important: this response works **only** for businesses and institutions. I would strongly advise never following up with individuals at their homes. It's creepy, and they may call the police on you.

But if it is a business or institutional prospect, you want them to put a face with your name. When you follow up again later, they will really know who you are.

Whatever objections you encounter, hang in there. Don't give up on the first no you receive. My rule of thumb is to try to make them tell me no at least twice—maybe three times if I'm really pushing. No matter how many times they say no, I always ask for permission to check back with them later in the year; in most cases, I'll call them again next quarter. I do this because I am that certain that I can better their situation, and it's my duty to give them the chance to do business with me. There are no words that will take the place of believing with absolutely certainty that your services will reap great returns for the client. Therefore, don't spend all of your time polishing your closing skills. You don't have to be perfect; you just have to be real.

The more real you are, and the more you're having a conversation with someone, the less you will come across as a salesperson. As a result, the prospect will be less likely to put you in the pool of salespersons who bombard them with requests to subscribe to a newspaper, change their cell phone service, or have their yard mowed. You don't want to be in the group telling someone to buy this or buy that. You are in a relationship business. You may think you're in the advisory business, but you're not. No matter what changes in your industry, your relationships with your clients secure your future. If you decide to switch firms or sell your practice, those relationships are your equity. This is why it's so important to treat every call as a chance to build a relationship, not to make a sale.

I've given you a system for determining the root causes of people's objections. Identifying where an objection comes from is more useful than being able to rattle off dozens of different rebuttals to people who don't want to do business with you anyway. The advisory industries have changed. Advisors are increasingly fulfilling a consultative role; the days of grabbing clients and forgetting about them are gone. The competition is too fierce, and information is too abundant. But if you can determine the cause of a prospect's objections, you can respond intelligently, gain their respect, and build a relationship.

6 QUESTIONS

If a prospect agrees to set a meeting right away, that's great! However, in many cases, they will ask questions to discover more about you and your practice. If that occurs, it is your opportunity to discuss your value, but more importantly, it's your chance to ask probing questions to find out more about them. Remember, most people's favorite topic is themselves; the more you get them talking, the more rapport you will build, and the more information you will have to tailor your meeting to their specific needs and wants.

Moreover, questions are a way to expose need, both to you and to the prospect. The selling process is a series of questions that lead a prospect to the desired result. Remember the example of asking someone what will happen if they eat doughnuts: it's more effective than telling them what will happen. In the same way, asking a prospect about their financial position and present investment strategies, or about their current insurance coverage, can lead them to formulate for themselves the answers you want. Here are some powerful questions that will help with your initial conversation and your meeting in person:

- What are your financial goals?
- How are you currently investing?
- What is your process for that? (Note: this is my favorite question. It's especially useful when people

tell you they handle their investments themselves.)

- Describe your perfect advisory relationship.
- How has your relationship with your current advisor been?
- What would you like to change about it?
- Are there any asset classes that you will be looking at in the next 24 months?
- Do you have a CPA or estate-planning attorney you enjoy working with?
- How would you describe your risk tolerance?
- What is your top priority for your investment portfolio?
- What does your current investment portfolio look like?
- Have you had a comprehensive financial plan done? Are you following it?
- Is there anything your current advisor could be doing better?
- Who else will be part of the decision-making process? (Note: it is very important to include everyone who will be making decisions.)
- Do you have any children going to college?
- Do you have any gift strategies for your children?
- When do you plan on retiring?
- Does your company have a retirement plan? Do you participate?
- Do you or your spouse contribute to an IRA or a Roth IRA?
- Do you have life and long-term healthcare insurance in place? When was the last time you reviewed them?

- Do you have a will or trust? When was the last time you reviewed it?
- Do you have a current mortgage?
- Do you have a home equity line of credit?
- Do you have any other investments outside of what we have discussed?

All of these questions are non-threatening and great for building rapport. They also help you uncover your prospect's concerns and beliefs. If you can use war stories or experiences with past or current clients, use them as examples in your dialogue. They will not only give you credibility, but also show your client that your interests are aligned with theirs.

One piece of advice: don't try to wedge these questions into the conversation. If you're not building rapport and it looks like you won't get a meeting out of it, don't just blindly lob a question in there. You will get nowhere by saying out of the blue, "The market is down; has your advisor contacted you lately?" Such abrupt questions (especially those that try to make a prospect verify that he or she has made a bad decision in their current advising relationship) will make you sound abrasive, thoughtless, and shady. You are a professional, and that should be part of your mindset.

7 BECOMING AND STAYING RELEVANT

We have covered many aspects of the initial cold call, but an equally important part of prospecting by phone is becoming and staying relevant to your clients. In this chapter we will explore how to do so through voicemails, follow-up, and maintaining your pipeline.

Voicemails

I'm always asked if I believe leaving voicemails is a good idea. There are advantages and disadvantages. The main advantage is that you will occasionally get a returned phone call that leads to meeting. Unfortunately, it can be quite rare, and the time you waste leaving voicemails is time that could be better spent reaching a live person on the phone. So my answer to this question is that it's all about feel. Prospecting by phone is a contact sport. The more time you spend engaging in meaningful conversations with prospects, the more success you'll have, so don't spend too much time with voicemails. However, if it's a prospect whom you really want to reach, leaving one or two voicemails will plant your name in their mind and give you the chance to mention a commonality such as a mutual acquaintance. At the same time, it could also irritate them. Whether to leave a voicemail is a judgment that only you can make, and it will vary, depending on the prospect.

However, if you decide to leave a voicemail, *do not* use it as an opportunity to pitch. Some people who write about sales recommend using voicemail as the chance to leave a miniature commercial. No guidance could be worse. (Think about the last time you received such a voicemail; did you listen till the end and marvel at what the salesperson had to say? No, you probably hung up immediately.) I recommend leaving only your name. By doing so, you prevent the prospect from refusing to return a sales call. I would suggest doing the same thing with gatekeepers. If they ask about the nature of the call, simply reply, "I'm with _____." That's it.

Let me give you a special bonus tip. If you strongly want to get ahold of someone, you can cut yourself off in a voicemail. Make it sound like the call has been dropped in the middle of your message; this creates intrigue and, in my experience, will get people to call you back about 70% of the time. For example, you could say, "Hi Bob, this is Scott Pace at (123) 456-7890. There's an issue that came up, and I'd like to…" Hang up mid-sentence. I have used this tactic sparingly in my career, but it's a good one to have up your sleeve when you're trying to get a very important person on the phone.

As I said, you have to use your best judgment when deciding whether to leave voicemails. For an institutional prospect, I would suggest leaving no more than one voicemail per week; on the second or third voicemail you don't have to say whom you're with. Whatever you do, don't irritate them with too many voicemails. You might call them every day, but keep the voicemails to a minimum.

The Fortune Is in the Follow-up

When following up, your main priority is, of course, to build rapport and make a friend; but once they know who you are, you want to become relevant. There are many ways to become and stay relevant to a prospect. For instance, you can:

- Call to offer research reports and updated market outlooks.
- Invite them to an educational seminar.
- Inform them of new lending rates.
- Inform them of changes in the tax code related to investments.
- Invite them to a sporting event.
- Invite them to a charity event.
- Send a copy of a news article that might be relevant to their business. If your client gets written up in the newspaper or a business journal, send them a hard copy of it with a congratulatory note.
- Let them know of a new service that you're providing to your clients.

Regardless of what kind of follow-up you do, tailor it to your prospect's interests. The closer it matches their objectives, the more relevant you and the information will be. And of course, at every opportunity, try to give them results in advance. Without giving away too much, offer to do something for them for free; you can share ideas that you're working on with other clients or give them access to research reports. Let them know you're there if they need a second opinion or a resource for any of their investment, insurance, trust, or lending needs.

The fortune is in the follow-up. It is where the real work begins, because most of the time you won't set a meeting on the first call. The greatest thing about the second, third, or fourth time you contact someone is that you now have a warm prospect. During my career in the financial services industry, I was always a little archaic in my methods; I kept hard sheets of paper on all prospects and took diligent notes on our conversations. For example, I would jot down that a prospect went to a conference or took a vacation. That way, when I followed up with them, I could remind them of our previous conversation by asking specific questions. I could also open the call by reminding them that they gave me permission to check back with them. This would help jog their memory and would increase the likelihood of setting a meeting.

If you've done your job at staying relevant, building great rapport and credibility, prospects will usually be more inclined to meet with you—not only for the first time, but for the second or third as well. However, if more than a year goes by after your initial meeting and the prospect has not made significant movements toward becoming a client, I highly recommend that you evaluate whether or not they are viable as a potential client. If you feel that they're not, it's okay to let them go and make room for someone else who needs your time and attention. This is my recommendation with any prospect. Nothing is more time-consuming or discouraging than when you feel like your efforts have been wasted on a person who has no intention of becoming a client or who has a decision-making disorder. However, if you've been asleep at the wheel and have not developed trust, credibility, and a sense of urgency, you may be the one to blame. Trust your intuition here, and be honest with yourself about why the prospect isn't moving forward.

The importance of follow-up cannot be overstated. I am not trying to close anyone on the first call. I'd like to, but it doesn't always happen. The first phone call is usually just a way to gain credibility and rapport; you don't want to sound like a salesperson reading a script. On the second call, you're friends. On the third, you're old friends, and they should book a meeting with you if they haven't already. Let them know that you will do whatever you can to meet with them.

When the time comes to book a meeting, be careful about suggesting specific days because that gives them an easy way to say no. Instead, say, "I'm in town Tuesday through Friday; what times do you have open?" Use this line even if you're in your home town; they don't know that you could have a demanding travel schedule. Don't show your cards. If you have to, tell them, "I'm available this week. I'm filling up my schedule, and you're the first call I've made. I've wanted to meet with you for a long time, so I called you first to give you top priority." This makes them feel special, and it forces *them* to tell *you* what days they can meet. And once an appointment is set, do not call to confirm; it only gives them the opportunity to back out.

The purpose of follow-up is to gain familiarity and establish a relationship with the prospect. At this point, you're no longer a cold caller. It's your opportunity to help them and to stay relevant. If you develop these relationships, they can last you a long time. If someone is rude when you call, don't do business with them; rude prospects make rude clients.

When you do get a meeting with a prospect, make sure you come armed with a stunning presentation. Guidance on how to create one is beyond the scope of this book, but if you'd like help with presentations, visit our website at advisorgrowth.com or call our office.

Pipeline

A great pipeline is important because, in addition to

feeding your business, it helps you stay relevant to the right kinds of prospects. By staying focused on the prospects who are most motivated to do business with you in the near future, you will have a system in place to keep anyone from falling through the cracks.

I've already mentioned "indications of interest"—a term that many advisors use, but one that I consider no different from "prospects." It is crucial to collapse the two categories into one, because they are fundamentally the same; they are both people with whom you believe you may do business in the future. When you erase the distinction between them, the folly of keeping huge lists of "indications of interest" becomes clear. Would you ever say that you had 1,000 prospects?

When an advisor tells me they have generated 1,000–5,000 indications of interest, all that means to me is that 1,000–5,000 people were too polite to hang up on them. They have filled their pipeline with an unmanageable number of both qualified and non-qualified prospects. In my opinion, the optimal number of prospects in an efficient pipeline is 100–150 individuals or households. The amount of time required to stay relevant to more than 1,000 individuals or households leaves no time to search for viable prospects who may be ready to do business today. So when building your pipeline, choose well. It is the lifeblood of your business, and the last time I checked, indications of interest don't pay the bills.

If you already have a huge pipeline, go through the list and be ruthlessly honest with yourself about which prospects have the potential to become clients. Pipelines are like statistics: when you put garbage in, you get garbage out. There's nothing noble about having a large pipeline filled with prospects who have no intention of becoming clients. I would rather have a pipeline of ten well-qualified prospects who are sure to convert in the next six months than to have over 1,000 people about whom I know nothing. Categorize your prospects according to the 1–4 system we discussed earlier.

But as you purify your pipeline, **never quit prospecting**. I see too many advisors focus all their energy on closing business that's about to come to fruition. They neglect to maintain their pipelines and then find themselves with a complete lack of new, viable prospects. This can cause advisors to lose months of production; it puts them on a rollercoaster ride of new business and no business. Heed my warning: never stop prospecting.

8 CONCLUSION

Building a multi-million dollar practice requires a dedication to actively marketing your services. Cold calling is one of the most effective and cost-efficient ways to do it. It is a fundamental method for establishing a successful practice; when you're new and lack resources, cold calling provides a great way to start. Every advisory practice should have three to five marketing campaigns running at all times. Whether they be referrals and introductions, seminars, centers of influence, networking, etc., you will find that your telephone skills play a part in all of them.

Every aspect of your practice should always be centered around the client's experience: your marketing, your practice management, your product and service offerings, as well as your commitment to constant and never-ending improvement of your skills as an advisor. That includes having a marvelous sales presentation. No matter how good you are on the phone, if you get in front of a prospect without a solid presentation, you have wasted your time. But the specifics of presentation mastery are the subject of another book.

Cold calling is an art, one that has to be learned and practiced. If you apply the lessons from this book, it will dramatically curtail your learning curve. Every part of the process is important, from your set-up and mindset to NLP, scripts, objections, questions, follow-up, and pipeline management. Adapt the scripts I've given you as needed, but you may find that you're most successful when you go off-script and just start talking to people. Always maintain the objective of booking an appointment, but if you don't get an appointment, don't give up. You can call back later as a warm caller, and you now have the tools to identify the root causes of, and how best to respond to, any objections they may raise.

So many advisors shudder at the thought of cold calling; I hope this book will prevent you from mentally defeating yourself before you begin. Every business that I have ever built, I have started through cold calling. It is an essential skill because no matter how successful you are, you will always be cold calling. You will always need to reach out to people with whom you have never spoken, even if they are leads that have been slightly warmed through referrals.

I spent 20 years with my office door closed and my scripts locked away. I didn't let anyone watch me do my magic, and now I've shared it with you. I hope everything in this book will help you become even more successful than I was. If you'd like more information about Advisor Growth's coaching, training, and other services, visit advisorgrowth.com.

Keep practicing and become a cold calling machine. I close with my favorite quote, by Henry Wadsworth Longfellow:

> The heights by great men reached and kept
> Were not attained by sudden flight,
> But they, while their companions slept,
> Were toiling upwards in the night.

I look forward to hearing about your success.

ABOUT THE AUTHOR

Scott Pace, founder of Advisor Growth, has become one of the most sought-after business development experts and coaches in the financial services industry. He is known for helping advisors implement growth strategies that result in up to triple-digit percentage increases in their business, while adding to their quality of life. With years of experience on both the private client and institutional sides of financial services, Scott brings to his coaching a level of expertise that could only be acquired inside the business. He lives with his two daughters in Kansas City, Missouri. You can follow and contact Scott at advisorgrowth.com.